Steele

GU00985960

Lang**Syne**

PUBLISHING

WRITING *to* REMEMBER

WRITING *to* REMEMBER

79 Main Street, Newtongrange,
Midlothian EH22 4NA
Tel: 0131 344 0414   Fax: 0845 075 6085
E-mail: info@lang-syne.co.uk
www.langsyneshop.co.uk

Design by Dorothy Meikle
Printed by Ricoh Print Scotland
© Lang Syne Publishers Ltd 2013

ISBN 978-1-85217-476-7

Steele

MOTTO:
Always faithful
(or)
Always loyal.

CREST:
An eagle holding a serpent in its beak
(and)
The heads of two lions.

NAME variations include:
Steal
Steel
Steeles

Chapter one:

The origins of popular surnames

by George Forbes and Iain Gray

If you don't know where you came from, you won't know where you're going is a frequently quoted observation and one that has a particular resonance today when there has been a marked upsurge in interest in genealogy, with increasing numbers of people curious to trace their family roots.

Main sources for genealogical research include census returns and official records of births, marriages and deaths – and the key to unlocking the detail they contain is obviously a family surname, one that has been 'inherited' and passed from generation to generation.

No matter our station in life, we all have a surname – but it was not until about the middle of the fourteenth century that the practice of being identified by a particular surname became commonly established throughout the British Isles.

Previous to this, it was normal for a person to be identified through the use of only a forename.

But as population gradually increased and there were many more people with the same forename, surnames were adopted to distinguish one person, or community, from another.

Many common English surnames are patronymic in origin, meaning they stem from the forename of one's father – with 'Johnson,' for example, indicating 'son of John.'

It was the Normans, in the wake of their eleventh century conquest of Anglo-Saxon England, a pivotal moment in the nation's history, who first brought surnames into usage – although it was a gradual process.

For the Normans, these were names initially based on the title of their estates, local villages and chateaux in France to distinguish and identify these landholdings.

Such grand descriptions also helped enhance the prestige of these warlords and generally glorify their lofty positions high above the humble serfs slaving away below in the pecking order who had only single names, often with Biblical connotations as in Pierre and Jacques.

The only descriptive distinctions among the peasantry concerned their occupations, like 'Pierre the swineherd' or 'Jacques the ferryman.'

Roots of surnames that came into usage in England not only included Norman-French, but also Old French, Old Norse, Old English, Middle English, German, Latin, Greek, Hebrew and the Gaelic languages of the Celts.

The Normans themselves were originally Vikings, or 'Northmen', who raided, colonised and eventually settled down around the French coastline.

The had sailed up the Seine in their longboats in 900AD under their ferocious leader Rollo and ruled the roost in north eastern France before sailing over to conquer England in 1066 under Duke William of Normandy – better known to posterity as William the Conqueror, or King William I of England.

Granted lands in the newly-conquered England, some of their descendants later acquired territories in Wales, Scotland and Ireland – taking not only their own surnames, but also the practice of adopting a surname, with them.

But it was in England where Norman rule and custom first impacted, particularly in relation to the adoption of surnames.

This is reflected in the famous *Domesday Book*, a massive survey of much of England and Wales, ordered by William I, to determine who owned what, what it was worth and therefore how much they were liable to pay in taxes to the voracious Royal Exchequer.

Completed in 1086 and now held in the National Archives in Kew, London, 'Domesday' was an Old English word meaning 'Day of Judgement.'

This was because, in the words of one contemporary chronicler, "its decisions, like those of the Last Judgement, are unalterable."

It had been a requirement of all those English landholders – from the richest to the poorest – that they identify themselves for the purposes of the survey and for future reference by means of a surname.

This is why the *Domesday Book*, although written in Latin as was the practice for several centuries with both civic and ecclesiastical records, is an invaluable source for the early appearance of a wide range of English surnames.

Several of these names were coined in connection with occupations.

These include Baker and Smith, while Cooks, Chamberlains, Constables and Porters were to be found carrying out duties in large medieval households.

The church's influence can be found in names such as Bishop, Friar and Monk while the popular name of Bennett derives from the late fifth to mid-sixth century Saint Benedict, founder of the Benedictine order of monks.

The early medical profession is represented by Barber, while businessmen produced names that include Merchant and Sellers.

Down at the village watermill, the names that cropped up included Millar/Miller, Walker and Fuller, while other self-explanatory trades included Cooper, Tailor, Mason and Wright.

Even the scenery was utilised as in Moor, Hill, Wood and Forrest – while the hunt and the chase supplied names that include Hunter, Falconer, Fowler and Fox.

Colours are also a source of popular surnames, as in Black, Brown, Gray/Grey, Green and White, and would have denoted the colour of the clothing the person habitually wore or, apart from the obvious exception of 'Green', one's hair colouring or even complexion.

The surname Red developed into Reid, while

Blue was rare and no-one wanted to be associated with yellow.

Rather self-important individuals took surnames that include Goodman and Wiseman, while physical attributes crept into surnames such as Small and Little.

Many families proudly boast the heraldic device known as a Coat of Arms, as featured on our front cover.

The central motif of the Coat of Arms would originally have been what was borne on the shield of a warrior to distinguish himself from others on the battlefield.

Not featured on the Coat of Arms, but high-lighted on page three, is the family motto and related crest – with the latter frequently different from the central motif.

Adding further variety to the rich cultural heritage that is represented by surnames is the appearance in recent times in lists of the 100 most common names found in England of ones that include Khan, Patel and Singh – names that have proud roots in the vast sub-continent of India.

Echoes of a far distant past can still be found in our surnames and they can be borne with pride in commemoration of our forebears.

Chapter two:

Ancient bloodlines

A name with two main points of origin, 'Steele' and its equally popular spelling variant of 'Steel' has been present on British shores from earliest times and in Ireland since at least the seventeenth century.

One derivation is from the Old English *stiger*, denoting a stile or something that had to be climbed over, but the main derivation is from the Scandinavian baptismal name 'Staal', indicating 'son of Stall.'

'Staal', rendered in Middle English as 'Stele', came to denote not only someone who worked with metals but also descriptive of someone as strong, reliant and durable as steel.

The name is understood to have been introduced to Britain through descendants of a Norman warrior, Bigot de Loges, who had fought at the side of Duke William of Normandy at the battle of Hastings in 1066.

Rewarded with lands in Cheshire and becoming lords of the manor of Giddy Hall, near

Sandbach, Bigot de Loges's descendants at some stage adopted the name of Steele.

Intermarriage by the Normans with the native Anglo-Saxons means that many bearers of popular surnames found in England today such as Steele have a rich and heady brew of Celtic, Anglo-Saxon and Norman blood flowing through their veins.

This rich heritage stretches back to before those Germanic tribes who invaded and settled in the south and east of the island of Britain from about the early fifth century.

Known as the Anglo-Saxons, they were composed of the Jutes, from the area of the Jutland Peninsula in modern Denmark, the Saxons from Lower Saxony, in modern Germany and the Angles from the Angeln area of Germany.

It was the Angles who gave the name 'Engla land', or 'Aengla land' – better known as 'England.'

They held sway in what became known as England from approximately 550 AD to 1066, with the main kingdoms those of Sussex, Wessex, Northumbria, Mercia, Kent, East Anglia and Essex.

Whoever controlled the most powerful of these kingdoms was tacitly recognised as overall 'king' – one of the most noted being Alfred the Great, King of Wessex from 871 AD to 899 AD.

It was during his reign that the famous *Anglo-Saxon Chronicle* was compiled – an invaluable source of Anglo-Saxon history – while Alfred was designated in early documents as *Rex Anglorum Saxonum*, King of the English Saxons.

Other important Anglo-Saxon works include the epic *Beowulf* and the seventh century *Caedmon's Hymn*.

Through the Anglo-Saxons, the language known as Old English developed, later transforming from the eleventh century into Middle English.

The Anglo-Saxons meanwhile, had usurped the power of the indigenous Celtic Britons – who referred to them as 'Saeson' or 'Saxones.'

It is from this that the Scottish-Gaelic term for 'English people' of 'Sasannach' derives, the Irish-Gaelic 'Sasanach' and the Welsh 'Saeson.'

We learn from the *Anglo-Saxon Chronicle* how the religion of the early Anglo-Saxons was one that pre-dated the establishment of Christianity in the British Isles.

Known as a form of Germanic paganism, with roots in Old Norse religion, it shared much in common with the Druidic 'nature-worshipping' religion of the indigenous Britons.

It was in the closing years of the sixth century that Christianity began to take a hold in Britain, while by approximately 690 it had become the 'established' religion of Anglo-Saxon England.

The first serious shock to Anglo-Saxon control of England came in 789 in the form of sinister black-sailed Viking ships that appeared over the horizon off the island monastery of Lindisfarne, in the northeast of the country.

Lindisfarne was sacked in an orgy of violence and plunder, setting the scene for what would be many more terrifying raids on the coastline of not only England, but also Ireland and Scotland.

But the Vikings, or 'Northmen', in common with the Anglo-Saxons of earlier times, were raiders who eventually stayed – establishing, for example, what became Jorvik, or York, and the trading port of Dublin, in Ireland.

Through intermarriage, the bloodlines of the Anglo-Saxons also became infused with that of the Vikings.

But there would be another infusion of the blood of the 'Northmen' in the wake of the Norman

Conquest of 1066 – a key event in English history that sounded the death knell of Anglo-Saxon supremacy.

By 1066, England had become a nation with several powerful competitors to the throne.

In what were extremely complex family, political and military machinations, the English monarch was Harold II, who had succeeded to the throne following the death of Edward the Confessor.

But his right to the throne was contested by two powerful competitors – his brother-in-law King Harold Hardrada of Norway, in alliance with Tostig, Harold II's brother, and Duke William II of Normandy.

In what has become known as The Year of Three Battles, Hardrada invaded England and gained victory over the English king on September 20 at the battle of Fulford, in Yorkshire.

Five days later, however, Harold II decisively defeated his brother-in-law and brother at the battle of Stamford Bridge.

But Harold had little time to celebrate his victory, having to immediately march south from Yorkshire to encounter a mighty invasion force, led by Duke William of Normandy that had landed at Hastings, in East Sussex.

Harold's battle-hardened but exhausted force of Anglo-Saxon soldiers confronted the Normans on October 25th in a battle subsequently depicted on the Bayeux tapestry – a 23ft. long strip of embroidered linen thought to have been commissioned eleven years after the event by the Norman Odo of Bayeux.

It was at the top of Senlac Hill that Harold drew up a strong defensive position, building a shield wall to repel Duke William's cavalry and infantry.

The Normans suffered heavy losses, but through a combination of the deadly skill of their archers and the ferocious determination of their cavalry, eventually won the day.

Anglo-Saxon morale had collapsed on the battlefield as word spread through the ranks that Harold had been killed – the Bayeux Tapestry depicting this as having happened when the English king was struck by an arrow to the head.

Amidst the carnage of the battlefield, it was difficult to identify Harold – the last of the Anglo-Saxon kings.

Some sources assert William ordered his body to be thrown into the sea, while others state it was secretly buried at Waltham Abbey.

But what is known with certainty is that

William, in celebration of his great victory, founded Battle Abbey, near the site of the battle, ordering that the altar be sited on the spot where Harold was believed to have fallen.

William was declared King of England on December 25, and what followed was the complete subjugation of his Anglo-Saxon subjects.

Those Normans who had fought on his behalf were rewarded with the lands of Anglo-Saxons, many of whom sought exile abroad as mercenaries.

Within an astonishingly short space of time, Norman manners, customs and law were imposed on England – laying the basis for what subsequently became established 'English' custom and practice.

Chapter three:

Honours and distinction

Bearers of the Steele name have stamped their mark on the historical record of a number of nations.

Born in 1803 in Upper Creevagh, Co. Donegal and emigrating from Ireland to the United States at the age of 21, the Reverend David Steele studied theology in Pittsburgh and became licensed as a minister in Bush Creek, Ohio, of the Reformed Presbyterian Church of North America (RPCNA).

But bitter doctrinal disputes within the church led to Steele and others splitting from it and constituting the church known as the Reformed Presbytery.

The RPCNA, Steele had thundered, had "corrupted the doctrines and worship, and prostituted the government and discipline of the house of God."

He died in 1887, but his church survives to this day as the Reformed Presbyterian Church (Covenanted), with its adherents known as Steelites.

On the fields of battle, Frederick Steele was a prominent U.S. Army general of the American Civil War of 1861 to 1865.

Born in 1819 in Delhi, New York, he graduated from West Point in 1843 and served in the Mexican-American War of 1846 to 1848.

He was appointed a major in the 11th U.S. Infantry on the outbreak of the Civil War and also held a number of other senior command positions, while in September of 1863 he was in command of the U.S. Army of Arkansas that took Confederate-held Little Rock.

Also known for leading, from February of 1865 to May of that year, the contingent of African-American soldiers known as the Column from Pensacola, by the time the conflict ended he had attained the rank of major general.

He died in 1868, while there is a monument to him in Vicksburg National Military Park.

Not only seeing military action during the Boer War and the First World War but also serving as an officer of the North-West Mounted Police, better known as the Mounties, Sir Samuel Benfield Steele was born in 1848 in Purbrook, in what was then Canada West.

Of Scottish roots through his mother, he joined the Permanent Force Artillery, Canada's first regular army unit, in 1871 after having attended the Royal Military College of Canada.

He joined the newly formed Canadian North-West Mounted Police two years later and rose swiftly through its ranks.

It was in his capacity as commander at Fort Qu'Appelle, North-West Territories that in 1877 he met with Sitting Bull who, following his defeat of General Custer at the battle of the Little Bighorn in June of 1876 had fled with his fellow Sioux into Canada.

Steele met with him to negotiate the terms for his temporary refuge in Canada.

Later, and with the rank of superintendent, he was responsible for attempting to maintain the rule of law in what had become the near anarchy of the Klondike, Yukon, during the Klondike Gold Rush of 1897 to 1899.

Order was maintained, in large part due to a number of Steele's initiatives that included a stipulation that prospectors were not allowed to enter the Yukon without at least a ton of supplies to support them.

During the Second Boer War of 1899 to 1902, Steele returned to active military duty as commanding officer of the cavalry unit Strathcona's Horse, raised by the Canadian Pacific Railway tycoon Lord Strathcona.

During the First World War, and despite initial reservations about his age, he was given command of the 2nd Canadian Division that fought with distinction on the Western Front.

Knighted at the end of the conflict in 1918, he died only a few weeks later, aged 70, with the rank of major general.

Mount Steele, Canada's fifth-tallest mountain, is named in his honour.

Two bearers of the Steele name have been recipients of the Victoria Cross (VC), the highest award for valour in the face of enemy action for British and Commonwealth forces.

Born in 1891 in Springhead, Yorkshire, Thomas Steele had been a sergeant in the 1st Battalion, Seaforth Highlanders during the First World War when, in February of 1917 near Sanna-y-Mat, Mesopotamia, he performed a number of actions under heavy enemy fire that included manning a machine-gun until relieved.

Although severely wounded, he survived the action and died at the age of 87.

Born in 1892 in Exeter, Devon, Captain Gordon Steele was a British naval recipient of the VC.

He had been a Royal Navy lieutenant,

serving with the North Russia Relief Force in support of the White Russians opposed to the Bolshevik Revolution when he performed the actions for which he was honoured with the VC.

It was in August of 1919 at Kronstadt, while second-in-command of a motor boat, that he took control of the vessel after his captain was killed and launched successful torpedo attacks on two Russian battleships.

Later attaining the rank of captain and serving during the Second World War, he died in 1981.

One famous American bearer of the Steele name during the Second World War was John M. Steele, whose dramatic exploits is portrayed by the actor Red Buttons in the 1962 film *The Longest Day*.

Born in 1912 in Metropolis, Illinois, he had been a private in the 82nd Airborne that had parachuted into the area west of the French village of St-Mère Église on the eve of D-Day of June 6th, 1944.

Steele was among a number of paratroopers who were dropped in error directly over the village, and while many of his comrades were easily picked off by German troops as they fell to earth, his parachute lines became entangled in one of the steeples of the church.

Wounded, he dangled above the ground for two hours, pretending to be dead, before being taken prisoner.

But he managed to escape in the confusion and, joining a unit of the 3rd Battalion, 505th Parachute Infantry Regiment, helped to retake the village.

Awarded the Bronze Star for bravery in combat, before his death in 1969 he regularly re-visited the town – where a parachute with an effigy of Steele in his Airborne uniform hangs from the steeple.

The local tavern, *Auberge John Steele*, is also named in his honour.

From the battlefield to politics, Sir David Steel is the distinguished British Liberal Democrat politician born in 1938 in Kirkcaldy, Fife.

The son of a former Moderator of the General Assembly of the Church of Scotland, also named David Steel, he first became involved in Liberal politics while a student at Edinburgh University.

From this, he went on to hold a number of senior posts that include Leader of the Liberal Party from 1976 until its merger in 1988 with the Social Democratic Party to form the Liberal Democrats.

A former Member of Parliament (MP) for Roxburgh, Selkirk and Peebles and, when this Borders constituency was abolished, for Tweeddale, Ettrick and Lauderdale, he also served from 1999 to 2003 as Member of the Scottish Parliament (MSP) for Lothians.

It was during his time in the Scottish Parliament that the veteran politician, who had been an active campaigner for devolution, served as the Parliament's first Presiding Officer.

Elevated to the Peerage of the United Kingdom in 1997 as Baron Steel of Aikwood, of Ettrick Forest in the Scottish Borders, he was created a Knight of the Thistle in 2004 – the highest honour that the Queen can bestow in Scotland.

Chapter four:

On the world stage

Bearers of the Steele name and its equally popular spelling variant of Steel have achieved international acclaim.

Best known for her roles in a series of gothic horror films of the 1960s that have now achieved cult status, **Barbara Steele** is the English actress born in 1937 in Birkenhead, Cheshire.

Now hailed as a classic of the genre, her first major role was in Italian director Mario Bava's 1960 *Black Sunday*, while she also starred in a number of other horror films that include the 1961 *The Pit and the Pendulum*, the 1962 *The Horrible Dr Hitchcock* and the 1965 *Nightmare Castle*.

In Scotland, **Dawn Steele** is the actress born in 1975 in Glasgow.

A student at the Royal Scottish Academy of Music and Drama in her home city from 1994 to 1998, she is best known for her role as Lexie MacDonald from 1999 to 2004 in the BBC drama series *Monarch of the Glen*, while other television credits include *Sea of Souls* and *Wild at Heart*.

Also on screen, **Amy Steel**, born in 1960 in Pennsylvania, is the American actress who, in addition to film credits that include the 1981 *Friday the 13th Part 2* and the 1987 *Walk Like A Man*, is best known for roles in television series that include *Seven Brides for Seven Brothers*, *The A-Team*, *Chicago* and *JAG*.

Married for a time to the Swedish actress Anita Ekberg, **Anthony Steel** was the English actor whose film credits include the 1950 *The Wooden Horse*, the 1959 *Honeymoon*, the 1975 *The Story of O* and, from 1980, *The Monster Club*; he died in 2001.

A model and actress of both film and television, **Karen Steele**, born in 1931 in Honolulu and who died in 1968, starred in an impressive list of films that range from the 1957 *Decision at Sundown* to the 1966 *Cyborg 2087* and, from 1969, *The Happy Ending*.

Not only a comedian, newspaper columnist and author but also a political commentator and former member of the Socialist Workers Party, **Mark Steel** was born in 1960.

In addition to presenting British television series that include *The Mark Steel Solution*, he is also the author of books that include his 2003 *Vive La Revolution* and three books of autobiography.

Born in Ohio in 1908, **Gile Steele** was an Academy Award-winning Hollywood costume designer.

One of the first Academy nominees when the category for Best Costume Design was introduced in 1948 for his work on *The Emperor Waltz*, he won the award a year later for *The Heiress* and, two years before his death in 1952, for *Samson and Delilah*.

Bearers of the Steele name have also excelled in the highly competitive world of sport.

In the boxing ring, **Freddie Steele**, nicknamed "The Tacoma Assassin", was the boxer and film actor who held the title of Middleweight Champion of the World from 1936 to 1938.

Born Frederick Earle Burgett in 1912 in Seattle, his intricate boxing footwork, as a double for Errol Flynn, featured in the 1942 film *Gentleman Jim*, while film credits in his own right include the 1944 *Hail the Conquering Hero* and, from 1948, *I Walk Alone*.

An inductee of both the World Boxing Hall of Fame and the International Boxing Hall of Fame, he died in 1984.

In rowing, **Paul Steele**, born in 1957 in New Westminster, British Columbia, is the Canadian rower who, as a member of his country's men's eights team, won the gold medal at the 1984 Los Angeles Olympics.

In basketball and best known for being a member of the Portland Trail Blazers team that won the 1977 National Basketball Association (NBA) finals, **Larry Steele** is the talented guard born in 1949 in Gary, Indiana.

On the cricket pitch, **David Steele** is the retired international cricketer who played eight Test Matches for England.

Born in 1941 in Bradeley, Staffordshire and a county cricketer for Northamptonshire, he was voted BBC Sports personality of the Year in 1975 and, a year later, named one of *Wisden's* Cricketers of the Year.

A player for the Scotland national football team in 1923, **David Steele** was the wing half who played for teams that include St Mirren, Bristol Rovers and Preston North End.

Born in 1894 in Carluke, Lanarkshire, before his death in 1964 he also managed English teams that include Huddersfield Town and Bradford City.

Enjoying a successful footballing career not only in his native Scotland but also in England and the United States, **Jim Steele** is the centre back born in 1950 in Edinburgh.

Teams he played for include Hearts, Dundee and Southampton, while in the United States he played for the Washington Diplomats, Memphis Rogues and, in 1981, Chicago Sting.

The recipient of six caps for the England international team between 1936 and 1937, **Freddie Steele**, born in 1916 in Stoke-on-Trent and who died in 1976, was the football forward who played for teams that include Stoke City and Port Vale.

From sport to music, Thomas William Hicks, born in 1936 in Bermondsey, London is the veteran English entertainer better known by his stage name of **Tommy Steele**.

Considered Britain's first rock and roll star, it was while serving as a merchant seaman that his ship docked in the American port of Norfolk, Virginia. On leave ashore, he first heard the music of Buddy Holly – and this inspired him to pursue a career as a musician.

Along with his first band, The Steelmen, he enjoyed a hit in 1956 with *Rock with the Caveman*, while a string of further hits, including the 1957 *Singing the Blues*, followed.

Also a talented actor, he starred in a number of films that include the 1967 *Half a Sixpence* and the 1968 *Finian's Rainbow*.

As a writer, he is the author of a number of books that include the children's novel *Quincy*, adapted for film in 1979.

In contemporary music, **Cassie Steele** is the Canadian singer and actress born in Toronto in 1989.

With albums that include her 2005 *How Much for Happy* and the 2009 *Destructo Doll*, she is also known for her role of Manny Santos in the television serial *Degrassi: The Next Generation*.

Also in Canada, **Duane Steele** is the country music star who was a recipient in 2001 of the Canadian Country Music Award.

Born in Hines Creek, Alberta, his top-selling albums include the 2000 *I'll Be Alright* and the 2010 *Gas and Time*.

Also in country music, **Jeffrey Steele**, born Jeffrey Le Vasseur in 1961 in Burbank, California, was named Songwriter of the Year in 2003 by the Nashville Songwriters Association International.

The singer and songwriter, who has had hits in his own right with songs that include *She'd Give Anything* and *They Don't Make 'Em Like That Anymore*, has also written songs for other artists that include the 2006 Rascal Flatts hit *What Hurts the Most*.

In a different musical genre, **David "Shuffle" Steele**, born in 1960 on the Isle of Wight, is the English musician who throughout the 1980s and early 1990s was bass guitarist with the band Fine Young Cannibals.

In the creative world of the written word, **Danielle Steel** is the internationally best-selling romantic novelist and author of mainstream works born Danielle Fernandes Dominque Schuelein-Steel in New York City in 1947.

Her rather unusual given name stems from her German father, an immigrant to the United States, and her Portuguese mother.

Rated one of the best-selling authors of all time and, as of 2012, the best-selling author alive, more than 800 million copies of her books have been sold worldwide since the publication of her first novel, *Going Home*, in 1972.

An inductee of the California Hall of Fame, other novels – many of which have been adapted for television – include her 1978 *Now and Forever*, the 1992 *Jewels* and, from 2012, *Hotel Vendome*.

In the science fiction genre, Allen Mulherin Steele, better known as **Allen M. Steele**, is the award-winning author who has served on the board of both the Science Fiction and Fantasy Authors of America and the Space Frontier Foundation.

Born in 1958 in Nashville, his 1996 *The Death of Captain Future* won the Hugo Award for Best Novella, as did his 1998 *Where Angels Fear to Tread* and the 2011 *The Emperor of Mars*.

From science fiction to science fact, Jack Ellwood Steele, better known as **Jack E. Steele**, was the American medical doctor and U.S. Air Force officer who coined the term 'bionics.'

Born in 1924 in Lacon, Illinois, Steele, who died in 2009, qualified as a doctor while serving for a time in the U.S. Army, studying neuro-anatomy before leaving the army to join the U.S. Air Force in 1951.

Joining the Aerospace Medical Research Laboratory in 1953, he coined the term 'bionics' to describe the study of biological organisms to find solutions to engineering problems – now also known as biomimetics.

Returning to the realms of science fiction, his research captured the imagination of the novelist Martin Caidan, whose 1972 book *Cyborg* mentions Steele by name and later formed the basis of the popular television series *The Six Million Dollar Man*.